W9-BCT-439

Team Spirit

THE ST. LOUIS CARDINALS

BY
MARK STEWART

Content Consultant
James L. Gates, Jr.
Library Director
National Baseball Hall of Fame and Museum

NorwoodHouse Press
Chicago, Illinois

Norwood House Press
P.O. Box 316598
Chicago, Illinois 60631

For information regarding Norwood House Press, please visit our website at:
www.norwoodhousepress.com or call 866-565-2900.

All photos courtesy of AP Images—AP/Wide World Photos, Inc., except the following:
Getty Images (4, 10, 15); General Mills, Inc. (6 top, 20);
Author's Collection (6 bottom, 15, 23, 37 both, 39); John Klein (9, 22, 28);
Bowman Gum Co. (14); Red Heart Dog Food Co. (17);
Topps, Inc. (21, 34 top, 35 top left and right and bottom left, 40 both, 43);
D. Buchner & Co. (34 bottom left); Goudey Gum Co. (34 bottom right);
Matt Richman (48 top).
Special thanks to Topps, Inc.

Editor: Mike Kennedy
Designer: Ron Jaffe
Project Management: Black Book Partners, LLC.

Special thanks to Carol and Bob Mick.

Library of Congress Cataloging-in-Publication Data

Stewart, Mark, 1960-
The St. Louis Cardinals / by Mark Stewart ; content consultant James L. Gates, Jr.
p. cm. -- (Team spirit)
Summary: "Presents the history, accomplishments and key personalities of the Saint Louis Cardinals baseball team. Includes timelines, quotes, maps, glossary and websites"--Provided by publisher.
Includes bibliographical references and index.
ISBN-13: 978-1-59953-096-3 (library edition : alk. paper)
ISBN-10: 1-59953-096-1 (library edition : alk. paper)
1. St. Louis Cardinals (Baseball team)--History--Juvenile literature. I. Gates, Jr., James L. II. Title.
GV875.S3S77 2007
796.357'640977866--dc22

2006033025

Manufactured in the United States of America.

COVER PHOTO: The Cardinals are a picture of joy after the final out of the 2006 World Series.

Table of Contents

SPORTS WORDS & VOCABULARY WORDS: In this book, you will find many words that are new to you. You may also see familiar words used in new ways. The glossary on page 46 gives the meanings of baseball words, as well as "everyday" words that have special baseball meanings. These words appear in **bold type** throughout the book. The glossary on page 47 gives the meanings of vocabulary words that are not related to baseball. They appear in ***bold italic type*** throughout the book.

PUJOLS
5
32
32
16

Meet the Cardinals

Long ago, when the United States was still a young country, the St. Louis Cardinals were baseball's westernmost team. They had fans from the Mississippi River to the Pacific Ocean. Today, there are many teams that play to the west of St. Louis, but the Cardinals still have fans for thousands of miles in every direction.

Rooting for the Cardinals is easy. They find players who understand the basics of baseball, and do the "little things" that often make the difference between winning and losing. That is one reason the Cardinals have won more championships than any team in the **National League (NL)**.

This book tells the story of the Cardinals. They are a team with a great past and an exciting future. They are also a team that players love to play for. Whether you are a superstar or a substitute, putting on a St. Louis uniform is not only a special thrill, it is one of baseball's greatest honors.

Chris Duncan is greeted by Adam Kennedy and Albert Pujols after a home run in 2007.

Way Back When

The city of St. Louis joined the National League in 1892, but its team was not a new one. For many years, the St. Louis Browns had ruled a rival league called the American Association. When that league went out of business, the team joined the NL. The team's owner, Chris von der Ahe, believed that baseball should be fun for fans. He built a carousel in the outfield, and staged boxing matches and horse races during games. He also held band contests in his ballpark, which he called the "***Coney Island*** of the West."

After a few years, von der Ahe sold the team. The new owners decided to change the look and the name of the club. The players' ***traditional*** brown stockings were replaced with cardinal-red socks. Some called the team the Perfectos, but soon they became known as the Cardinals. No matter what the name, it did not help them win games. For their first 34 seasons, the team did not finish higher than third place. Their best player during this time was second baseman Rogers Hornsby. He was a powerful hitter who won the batting championship six years in a row, and batted over .400 three times.

The Cardinals won their first **pennant** in 1926. By then Branch Rickey was running the team. He was the first person to build a farm system that "grew" young talent. In the early days of baseball, **minor-league** teams made money by selling their best players to **major-league** teams. Rickey paid the bills for a group of minor-league teams in exchange for their promise that they would send their best players to the Cardinals. Today, all major-league clubs have similar agreements.

With a steady stream of young stars, the Cardinals won the NL pennant nine times between 1926 and 1946. They had some of baseball's best players. The team's hitting stars included Joe Medwick, Frankie Frisch, Jim Bottomley, Chick Hafey, Pepper Martin, Johnny Mize, Stan Musial, Marty Marion, and Enos Slaughter. The Cardinals' top pitchers were Jesse Haines, Flint Rhem, Bill Sherdel, and Grover Cleveland Alexander. Their most colorful players were the Dean brothers, Jay and Paul—better known as "Dizzy" and "Daffy."

LEFT: Rogers Hornsby, who starred for the Cardinals in the early 1900s. **TOP RIGHT**: Jay "Dizzy" Dean, a great pitcher and teammate for the Cardinals. **BOTTOM RIGHT**: A Stan Musial pin from the 1940s.

Cardinals

After struggling in the 1950s, the Cardinals became one of the NL's best teams again. Led by pitcher Bob Gibson, catcher Tim McCarver, and outfielders Curt Flood and Lou Brock, St. Louis won three pennants between 1964 and 1968. The Cardinals won three more pennants during the 1980s, with a team known for its great speed and excellent defense. During those years, fans cheered for popular players such as Ozzie Smith, Willie McGee, Vince Coleman, and Tommy Herr.

More stars wore the Cardinals uniform during the 1990s, including Todd Zeile, Ray Lankford, Brian Jordan, Mark McGwire, and Matt Morris. However, despite having good managers and star players, the team did not return to the **World Series**. It would take a new generation of players to get the Cardinals back to the top of the **standings**.

LEFT: Bob Gibson, who led the Cardinals to two championships in the 1960s. He won 251 games during his career.
ABOVE: Mark McGwire, the team's top slugger during the 1990s.

ANKIEL
24
Cardinals
5

The Team Today

In 2001, the Cardinals took a great leap forward after an unknown minor leaguer named Albert Pujols made the team. He had been a ***professional*** player for only one year, but once he was given a chance in the major leagues, he hit like a superstar. Before long, Pujols, Jim Edmonds, and Scott Rolen formed the heart of baseball's most powerful **lineup**.

Pitching and defense are also important to the team's success. The Cardinals work hard to put together a team that does everything well. In 2006, they began playing in new Busch Stadium. The Cardinals celebrated by winning the World Series that year—their first championship since 1982.

The Cardinals have become very good at finding players with different skills, and blending them together in winning ways. That is why, at the beginning of most seasons, St. Louis is often the team to beat in the NL's **Central Division**.

Albert Pujols congratulates Rick Ankiel on a home run during the 2007 season.

FAMOUS-BARR
PARTY PORCH
Coca-Cola
Ford
YOU
Ameren
BUD LIGHT

Home Turf

Baseball has been an important part of city life in St. Louis for more than a century. In the 1890s, the team played on a field that was surrounded by a popular amusement park and concert area. Starting in 1920, the Cardinals played in Sportsman's Park. They shared it with the city's **American League (AL)** team, the Browns—a club that began play in 1902 and "borrowed" the Cardinals' old team name.

In 1966, the Cardinals moved into Busch Stadium, a modern park that ***favored*** pitching and defense. The team celebrated its new home with a World Series championship in 1967. In 2006, the Cardinals moved into a new Busch Stadium, which was built right next to the old one. It mixes old-time charm with many modern features, and has wonderful views of the famous St. Louis Gateway Arch and the downtown skyline.

BY THE NUMBERS

- *The stadium has 46,861 seats.*
- *The cost of the new stadium was $365 million.*
- *The distance from home plate to the left field foul pole is 336 feet.*
- *The distance from home plate to the center field fence is 400 feet.*
- *The distance from home plate to the right field foul pole is 335 feet.*

The new Busch Stadium is located in the heart of St. Louis.

Dressed for Success

The Cardinals are not named after the well-known red bird. Originally, the team's nickname came from the cardinal-red color of the St. Louis uniform. Not until 1918 did "Cardinals" appear on the players' jerseys. Four years later, the team started wearing uniforms with two birds perched on a sloping baseball bat. The ***interlocking*** *S–T–L* on the Cardinals' cap was first used around 1900.

Over the years, there have been small changes made to the Cardinals' cap and uniform. During the 1950s, the birds and bat disappeared for a few years. In the 1970s, the team wore light blue for several seasons instead of white. The look of the Cardinals' cap has also changed from time to time, but their overall uniform is still one of baseball's most traditional.

Del Rice models a St. Louis uniform from the early 1950s.

UNIFORM BASICS

The baseball uniform has not changed much since the Cardinals began playing. It has four main parts:

- a cap or batting helmet with a sun visor
- a top with a player's number on the back
- pants that reach down between the ankle and the knee
- stirrup-style socks

The uniform top sometimes has a player's name on the back. The team's name, city, or ***logo*** is usually on the front. Baseball teams wear light-colored uniforms when they play at home, and darker styles when they play on the road.

For more than 100 years, baseball uniforms were made of wool ***flannel*** and were very baggy. This helped the sweat ***evaporate*** and gave players the freedom to move around. Today's uniforms are made of ***synthetic*** fabrics that stretch with players and keep them dry and cool.

Adam Wainwright fires a pitch in the team's 2007 home uniform.

We Won!

The Cardinals were the most successful team in the NL from the mid-1920s to the mid-1940s. During that time, they won nine pennants and six World Series. Their first championship came against Babe Ruth and the powerful New York Yankees in 1926. In Game Seven of that series, 39-year-old Grover Cleveland Alexander pitched in relief and saved the day for the Cardinals—after he had pitched a **complete game** the day before!

The Cardinals were known as the "Gas House Gang" during the 1930s. They had a group of tough, talented players who liked to win and loved to have fun. They captured the pennant three times in five seasons, and won the World Series in 1931 and 1934. Both times, the Cardinals won exciting seventh games. The star of the '31 World Series was the daring Pepper

Martin, who stole five bases and batted .500. The star of the '34 World Series was Dizzy Dean, who pitched a **shutout** in the final game.

St. Louis reached the World Series four more times during the 1940s. This team was led by a group of young stars, including Stan Musial, Enos Slaughter, Marty Marion, Terry Moore, Mort Cooper, and Harry Brecheen. The Cardinals beat the Yankees in 1942, the Browns in 1944, and the Boston Red Sox in 1946. In the victory over the Red Sox, the speedy Slaughter scored all the way from first base on a long single to win the final game. It is one of baseball's most famous plays.

The Cardinals won three more pennants during the 1960s. They beat the Yankees in the 1964 World Series and defeated the Red Sox in 1967. St. Louis was ahead of the Tigers three games to one in the 1968 World Series, but Detroit made a great ***comeback*** to win. Pitcher Bob Gibson and outfielder Lou Brock starred for the Cardinals in all three

LEFT: Pepper Martin and Dizzy Dean, two of the leaders of the "Gas House Gang." **ABOVE**: Enos Slaughter, whose daring baserunning won the 1946 World Series.

of these action-packed, seven-game series. Other World Series heroes included Tim McCarver, Ken Boyer, Roger Craig, Nelson Briles, Julian Javier, and Orlando Cepeda.

The next time the Cardinals reached the World Series, in 1982, they defeated the Milwaukee Brewers in seven exciting games. The Cardinals needed a full team effort to win, and manager Whitey Herzog made some clever decisions about whom to put in the games. Many players had great moments during this series, including pitchers Joaquin Andujar and Bruce Sutter, **rookie** Willie McGee, and veterans George Hendrick, Keith Hernandez, and Dane Iorg. St. Louis trailed Milwaukee three games to two, but won the last two games 13–1 and 6–3. It was the team's ninth championship.

The Cardinals won their tenth championship in 2006. During that season, almost every one of the team's stars missed time because of injuries. The players who filled their shoes gained good experience, and did well enough for the Cardinals to win the NL Central. During the playoffs and World Series, they continued to help the team as it beat the San Diego Padres, New York Mets, and Detroit Tigers.

The amazing hitting of Yadier Molina, Scott Spezio, and David Eckstein made the difference on offense. Jeff Suppan, Jeff Weaver, and Adam Wainwright were the pitching stars. St. Louis beat Detroit four games to one to win the championship. Weaver and Wainwright teamed up to win the final game, and Eckstein was named the World Series **Most Valuable Player (MVP)**.

LEFT: Catcher Tim McCarver rushes to hug Ken Boyer and Bob Gibson after the final out of the 1964 World Series. **ABOVE**: Yadier Molina and Adam Wainwright celebrate the final out of the 2006 World Series.

Go-To Guys

To be a true star in baseball, you need more than a quick bat and a strong arm. You have to be a "go-to guy"—someone the manager wants on the pitcher's mound or in the batter's box when it matters most. Cardinals fans have had a lot to cheer about over the years, including these great stars …

THE PIONEERS

ROGERS HORNSBY — Second Baseman

• BORN: 4/27/1896 • DIED: 1/5/1963 • PLAYED FOR TEAM: 1915 TO 1926 & 1933

Many experts believe that Rogers Hornsby was the best right-handed hitter in history. He won the NL batting championship each year from 1920 to 1925, and was the **player-manager** of the Cardinals when they won the 1926 World Series.

JOE MEDWICK — Outfielder

• BORN: 11/24/1911 • DIED: 3/21/1975

• PLAYED FOR TEAM: 1932 TO 1940 & 1947 TO 1948

If Joe Medwick liked a pitch, he hit it hard whether it was a ball or a strike. In 1937, he won the **Triple Crown**—no NL player has won it since.

ABOVE: Joe Medwick **RIGHT**: Lou Brock

DIZZY DEAN **Pitcher**

• BORN: 1/16/1910 • DIED: 7/17/1974 • PLAYED FOR TEAM: 1930 & 1932 TO 1937

Dizzy Dean was the best pitcher in baseball for five seasons during the 1930s. In 1934, he won 30 games. In 1936, he won 24 and **saved** 11 more. Dean threw a sizzling fastball with an easy motion, and also had a great **changeup**.

STAN MUSIAL **Outfielder/First Baseman**

• BORN: 11/21/1920 • PLAYED FOR TEAM: 1941 TO 1944 & 1946 TO 1963

Stan "The Man" Musial was the best hitter in the NL during the 1940s and 1950s. Musial was the first player to play 1,000 games at two different positions.

BOB GIBSON **Pitcher**

• BORN: 11/9/1935 • PLAYED FOR TEAM: 1959 TO 1975

There was no greater competitor in baseball than Bob Gibson. He pitched in nine World Series games and won seven of them, with 92 strikeouts and a 1.89 **earned run average (ERA)**. Gibson won three games in the 1967 World Series, and won the NL **Cy Young Award** in 1968 and 1970.

LOU BROCK **Outfielder**

• BORN: 6/18/1939

• PLAYED FOR TEAM: 1964 TO 1979

Lou Brock was a powerful hitter and fast baserunner. He led the NL in stolen bases eight times, including 118 in 1974.

MODERN STARS

TED SIMMONS — Catcher

• BORN: 8/9/1949 • PLAYED FOR TEAM: 1968 TO 1980

If Ted Simmons could walk, he would play. He was a tough competitor who ignored injuries and batted .300 six times for the Cardinals.

KEITH HERNANDEZ — First Baseman

• BORN: 10/20/1953 • PLAYED FOR TEAM: 1974 TO 1983

Keith Hernandez was baseball's best defensive first baseman when he played for the Cardinals. In 1979, he hit .344 and was the league's co-MVP with **Hall of Famer** Willie Stargell.

OZZIE SMITH — Shortstop

• BORN: 12/26/1954

• PLAYED FOR TEAM: 1982 TO 1996

When Ozzie Smith came to the Cardinals in a trade with the San Diego Padres, he was known as a great fielder. The "Wizard of Oz" became an excellent hitter and base-stealer in St. Louis. He led the team to three pennants.

LEFT: Ozzie Smith
RIGHT: Albert Pujols

WILLIE McGEE **Outfielder**

• BORN: 11/2/1958 • PLAYED FOR TEAM: 1982 TO 1990 & 1996 TO 1999

Sleepy-eyed, ***pigeon-toed*** Willie McGee did not look like an **All-Star**, but he played like one. He won three **Gold Glove** awards, two batting championships, and was the star of the 1982 World Series.

JIM EDMONDS **Outfielder**

• BORN: 6/27/1970

• PLAYED FOR TEAM: 2000 TO 2007

The Cardinals have had many great center fielders, but none better than Jim Edmonds. He won the Gold Glove in each of his first six seasons with the team, and hit over 40 home runs in 2000 and 2004.

ALBERT PUJOLS **First Baseman**

• BORN: 1/16/1980

• FIRST YEAR WITH TEAM: 2001

Few fans had heard of Albert Pujols when he first became a Cardinal. Within a few years, he was being called the best young hitter in baseball. Pujols won the batting championship at the age of 23, and led the NL in runs three seasons in a row.

On the Sidelines

The Cardinals believe that a good manager understands his players as well as he understands the game. This allows him to get the most out of the talent he puts on the field. Over the years, the Cardinals have had many excellent leaders, including Miller Huggins, Gabby Street, Frankie Frisch, Billy Southworth, Red Schoendienst, Whitey Herzog, and Joe Torre.

Branch Rickey managed St. Louis during the 1920s. He is best known for his work in the 1930s, however. Rickey made agreements with many minor-league teams to help develop the young players that the Cardinals signed. This became known as a farm system. During the 1930s, the Cardinals had 32 different farm teams.

In 1996, the Cardinals hired Tony La Russa, one of the smartest managers in history. He used his knowledge of baseball to build a team that could win in many different ways. The Cardinals finished first in their division seven times in La Russa's first 11 seasons.

Tony La Russa gives encouragement to pitcher Anthony Reyes with a pat on the back.

One Great Day

OCTOBER 15, 1946

The 1946 World Series was a special one for baseball fans. For four years, the game's greatest stars had been fighting in World War II. Now, every team was back at full strength. The Cardinals won the NL championship after a thrilling pennant race. The Boston Red Sox took the AL pennant by 12 games. They looked unbeatable when the World Series began.

The Cardinals quickly showed that they were every bit as good as Boston. The series seesawed back and forth until it reached Game Seven in St. Louis. The Red Sox scored first, but the Cardinals came back to take a 3–1 lead. The Red Sox would not give up. They scored two runs in the top of the eighth inning to tie the score.

Enos Slaughter began the bottom of the eighth inning for St. Louis with a single. After two Cardinals made outs, Harry Walker was sent to the plate as a pinch-hitter. He smashed a line drive to left-center field. Slaughter was already rounding second base when Boston outfielder Leon Culberson reached the ball. Slaughter was a fast and daring runner. He decided he would try to score.

Enos Slaughter slides home to complete his "Mad Dash" in Game Seven of the 1946 World Series.

Culberson threw to Johnny Pesky. Slaughter was just about to step on third base when Pesky caught the ball. The Boston shortstop had his back to the infield. He thought Slaughter would stop where he was. That's what Slaughter was hoping for. When Pesky saw Slaughter racing for the plate, he froze for a moment before throwing to the catcher. By the time the ball arrived at home plate, it was too late. Slaughter had scored the go-ahead run.

St. Louis now led 4–3. The Red Sox were unable to score in the ninth inning. The Cardinals were world champions. More than 60 years later, St. Louis fans still talk about Slaughter's "Mad Dash"—and Boston fans still wonder how he made it all the way home from first base.

Legend Has It

Was Brian Jordan the Cardinals' greatest "two-sport" star?

LEGEND HAS IT that he was. The team has had a number of athletes who were successful in other sports, including first baseman George Crowe, who played professional basketball in the 1940s. Before Jordan joined St. Louis in 1992, he was a star ***defensive back*** for the Atlanta Falcons of the National Football League.

Was Curt Flood the "father" of free agency?

LEGEND HAS IT that he was. In 1970, Flood refused to be traded by the Cardinals to the Philadelphia Phillies. The All-Star outfielder claimed that he had earned the right to decide which team he would play for. His court case about this issue helped create the free agency system that players enjoy today. A free agent is a player who is allowed to play for any team that wants him.

Who was the first woman to run a major-league team?

LEGEND HAS IT that it was Helen Britton. She took over the Cardinals in 1911 after her uncle, owner Stanley Robison, passed away. How did she do? The team had its first winning season in 10 years and made more money than ever before.

LEFT: Brian Jordan **ABOVE**: Curt Flood

It Really Happened

The Cardinals had a very good pitching staff in 1966. Bob Gibson, Steve Carlton, Nelson Briles, Ray Washburn, and Joe Hoerner were among the toughest pitchers in baseball. These players would help the Cardinals win the pennant in 1967 and 1968. In 1966, however, the Los Angeles Dodgers were champions of the league.

The Dodgers were not scared of anyone that season, except Larry Jaster. He was a 22-year-old left-hander who had pitched just four games for the Cardinals the year before. Jaster played against Los Angeles five times in 1966, and each time the Dodgers failed to score a run. No one had ever pitched five shutouts in a row against the same team in the same season, and no one has done it since.

Jaster's record in 1966 was 5–0 against the Dodgers, and only 6–5 against other teams. His ERA against the Dodgers was 0.00 in 45 innings pitched, and more than 4.00 against everyone else. No one—not even Jaster himself—can explain his success against the Dodgers. He simply threw the ball over the plate, and the Los Angeles hitters could not score a run.

Larry Jaster gets a pitching tip from coach Howie Pollet.

Cardinals
42
Cardinals
4
70

Team Spirit

Every team believes that its fans are the most loving and loyal in baseball. For more than 100 years, the people of St. Louis have backed their team in the best of times and the worst of times. That is why, when players are asked to "rate" the fans, they often choose the Cardinals' fans. The crowds in St. Louis know the game, and they cheer for good plays, no matter which team makes them.

People travel to see the team from all over the Midwest. Many buy tickets for three or four games, and create a family vacation around a Cardinals' **homestand**. St. Louis fans show their support by wearing team colors to the games. From the rooftops of nearby Clark Street, Busch Stadium looks like a sea of red!

No one is redder than the team's beloved mascot, Fredbird. During games, he roams the field and visits with fans in the stands. He also stops by Fredbird Field, a play area for kids that is a favorite part of Busch Stadium.

Fredbird gets fans excited and keeps them laughing with his funny antics.

Timeline

Rogers Hornsby

1892
The team joins the NL and is managed by its owner, Chris von der Ahe.

1924
Rogers Hornsby sets a modern record with a .424 batting average.

1926
The Cardinals win their first championship.

1934
Player-manager Frankie Frisch leads the Cardinals to their third championship.

1944
The Cardinals defeat the city's AL team, the Browns, in the World Series.

Chris von der Ahe

Frankie Frisch

Bob Gibson

Vince Coleman

1963
Stan Musial retires as the NL's all-time leader in hits, with 3,630.

1968
Bob Gibson pitches 13 shutouts and finishes the year with a 1.12 ERA.

1979
Garry Templeton becomes the first **switch-hitter** with 100 hits from each side of the plate in the same season.

1985
Vince Coleman steals 110 bases in his rookie season.

1998
Mark McGwire becomes the first player in history to hit 70 home runs in one season.

2006
The Cardinals win their 10th World Series.

Stan Musial

So Taguchi and World Series MVP David Eckstein celebrate their victory over the Detroit Tigers.

Fun Facts

FLIPPED OUT

Ozzie Smith had many memorable moments during his career with the Cardinals, yet he is best known for something he did before games even started. Smith would run toward his position and do a flip, landing right on his feet.

QUICK SWITCH

In 1922, the Cardinals and Cubs made a trade between games of a **doubleheader**. Max Flack walked from the Chicago locker room to the St. Louis locker room, and Cliff Heathcote did the same in the opposite direction.

BROTHERS IN ARMS

Before the 1934 season, Dizzy Dean promised that he and his brother, Paul, would win 45 games for the Cardinals. Fans thought he was just being funny, but the Deans had the last laugh. Dizzy won 30 times and Paul won 19 times.

MR. PRESIDENT

Bill White, who played seven seasons for the Cardinals in the 1960s, became president of the National League after he retired from baseball.

G'DAY, MATE

During the 1890s, the team's second baseman was Joe Quinn. He was the first Australian player in major-league history.

JACK IN THE BOOTH

For nearly 50 seasons, fans in and around St. Louis followed the Cardinals through the voice of the team, Jack Buck. Listening to the smart, good-natured announcer was like visiting with an old friend. After each victory, Buck would say, "That's a winner!"

WELCOME TO THE MAJORS

In 2000, two Cardinals—Keith McDonald and Chris Richard—each hit a home run in his first major-league at bat. The last Cardinal to do this was Wally Moon, in 1954.

TOP LEFT: Ozzie Smith
BOTTOM LEFT: Paul and Dizzy Dean
TOP RIGHT: Bill White
BOTTOM RIGHT: Keith McDonald

Talking Baseball

"I'm a baseball player. I'm also a guy who mows his lawn and plays with his dog."

—Scott Rolen, on why he does not act like a star

"We've got the best fans in St. Louis. A lot of people want to come and play in St. Louis because of the way fans treat us."

—Albert Pujols, on the crowds at Busch Stadium

"I love to play this game of baseball. I love to put on this uniform."

—Stan Musial, on why he played 24 seasons with the Cardinals

"I've always had to win. I've *got* to win."

—Bob Gibson, on what made him such a great competitor

"There is no greater pleasure in the world than walking up to the plate with men on base and knowing that you are feared."

—Ted Simmons, on being a respected hitter

"Too many kids get discouraged over physical errors … but it's the mental errors they should worry about. Like throwing to the wrong base and making baserunning ***blunders***."

—Ken Boyer, on how young players can improve

"I have never seen a team more talented than ours was."

—Curt Flood, on the 1967 and 1968 Cardinals

LEFT: Scott Rolen and Albert Pujols
ABOVE: George Crowe, Ken Boyer, and Curt Flood (#21) chat and enjoy some coffee. The Cardinals were known for having an especially relaxed and friendly locker room.

For the Record

The great Cardinals teams and players have left their marks on the record books. These are the "best of the best" …

Ken Boyer

Joe Torre

CARDINALS AWARD WINNERS

WINNER	AWARD	YEAR
Frankie Frisch	Most Valuable Player	1931
Dizzy Dean	Most Valuable Player	1934
Joe Medwick	Most Valuable Player	1937
Mort Cooper	Most Valuable Player	1942
Stan Musial	Most Valuable Player	1943
Marty Marion	Most Valuable Player	1944
Stan Musial	Most Valuable Player	1946
Stan Musial	Most Valuable Player	1948
Wally Moon	Rookie of the Year*	1954
Bill Virdon	Rookie of the Year	1955
Ken Boyer	Most Valuable Player	1964
Orlando Cepeda	Most Valuable Player	1967
Bob Gibson	Most Valuable Player	1968
Bob Gibson	Cy Young Award	1968
Bob Gibson	Cy Young Award	1970
Joe Torre	Most Valuable Player	1971
Bake McBride	Rookie of the Year	1974
Keith Hernandez	co-Most Valuable Player	1979
Willie McGee	Most Valuable Player	1985
Vince Coleman	Rookie of the Year	1985
Whitey Herzog	Manager of the Year	1985
Todd Worrell	Rookie of the Year	1986
Albert Pujols	Rookie of the Year	2001
Tony La Russa	Manager of the Year	2002
Albert Pujols	Most Valuable Player	2005
Chris Carpenter	Cy Young Award	2005

** The Rookie of the Year award is given to the league's best first-year player.*

CARDINALS ACHIEVEMENTS

ACHIEVEMENT	YEAR
NL Pennant Winner	1926
World Series Champions	1926
NL Pennant Winner	1928
NL Pennant Winner	1930
NL Pennant Winner	1931
World Series Champions	1931
NL Pennant Winner	1934
World Series Champions	1934
NL Pennant Winner	1942
World Series Champions	1942
NL Pennant Winner	1943
NL Pennant Winner	1944
World Series Champions	1944
NL Pennant Winner	1946
World Series Champions	1946
NL Pennant Winner	1964
World Series Champions	1964
NL Pennant Winner	1967
World Series Champions	1967
NL Pennant Winner	1968
NL Pennant Winner	1982
World Series Champions	1982
NL Pennant Winner	1985
NL Pennant Winner	1987
NL Pennant Winner	2004
NL Pennant Winner	2006
World Series Champions	2006

ABOVE: Lou Brock flashes a big smile after the Cardinals' victory in Game One of the 1967 World Series. St. Louis won in seven games.
RIGHT: Stan Musial, who won three MVPs and led the Cardinals to four pennants.

Pinpoints

The history of a baseball team is made up of many smaller stories. These stories take place all over the map—not just in the city a team calls "home." Match the pushpins on these maps to the Team Facts and you will begin to see the story of the Cardinals unfold!

TEAM FACTS

Tim McCarver

1 St. Louis, Missouri—*The team has played here since 1892.*
2 Donora, Pennsylvania—*Stan Musial was born here.*
3 Carteret, New Jersey—*Joe Medwick was born here.*
4 Roxboro, North Carolina—*Enos Slaughter was born here.*
5 Jacksonville, Florida—*Vince Coleman was born here.*
6 Mobile, Alabama—*Ozzie Smith was born here.*
7 Memphis, Tennessee—*Tim McCarver was born here.*
8 Omaha, Nebraska—*Bob Gibson was born here.*
9 San Francisco, California—*Willie McGee was born here.*
10 Santo Domingo, Dominican Republic—*Albert Pujols was born here.*
11 Ponce, Puerto Rico—*Orlando Cepeda was born here.*
12 Sydney, Australia—*Joe Quinn was born here.*

Play Ball

Baseball is a game played between two teams over nine innings. Teams take one turn at bat and one turn in the field during each inning. A turn at bat ends when three outs are made. The batters on the hitting team try to reach base safely. The players on the fielding team try to prevent this from happening.

In baseball, the ball is controlled by the pitcher. The pitcher must throw the ball to the batter, who decides whether or not to swing at each pitch. If a batter swings and misses, it is a strike. If the batter lets a good pitch go by, it is also a strike. If the batter swings and the ball does not stay in fair territory (between the v-shaped lines that begin at home plate) it is called "foul," and is counted as a strike. If the pitcher throws three strikes, the batter is out. If the pitcher throws four bad pitches before that, the batter is awarded first base. This is called a base-on-balls, or "walk."

When the batter swings the bat and hits the ball, everyone springs into action. If a fielder catches a batted ball before it hits the ground, the batter is out. If a fielder scoops the ball off the ground and throws it to first base before the batter arrives, the batter is out. If the batter reaches first base safely, he is credited with a hit. A one-base hit is called a single, a two-base hit is called a double, a three-base hit is called a triple, and a four-base hit is called a home run.

Runners who reach base are only safe when they are touching one of the bases. If they are caught between the bases, the fielders can tag them with the ball and record an out.

A batter who is able to circle the bases and make it back to home plate before three outs are made is credited with a run scored. The team with the most runs after nine innings is the winner.

Anyone who has played baseball (or softball) knows that it can be a complicated game. Every player on the field has a job to do. Different players have different strengths and weaknesses. The pitchers, batters, and managers make hundreds of decisions every game. The more you play and watch baseball, the more "little things" you are likely to notice. The next time you are at a game, look for these plays:

PLAY LIST

DOUBLE PLAY—A play where the fielding team is able to make two outs on one batted ball. This usually happens when a runner is on first base, and the batter hits a ground ball to one of the infielders. The base runner is forced out at second base and the ball is then thrown to first base before the batter arrives.

HIT AND RUN—A play where the runner on first base sprints to second base while the pitcher is throwing the ball to the batter. When the second baseman or shortstop moves toward the base to wait for the catcher's throw, the batter tries to hit the ball to the place that the fielder has just left. If the batter swings and misses, the fielding team can tag the runner out.

INTENTIONAL WALK—A play when the pitcher throws four bad pitches on purpose, allowing the batter to walk to first base. This happens when the pitcher would much rather face the next batter—and is willing to risk putting a runner on base.

SACRIFICE BUNT—A play where the batter makes an out on purpose so that a teammate can move to the next base. On a bunt, the batter tries to "deaden" the pitch with the bat instead of swinging at it.

SHOESTRING CATCH—A play where an outfielder catches a short hit an inch or two above the ground, near the tops of his shoes. It is not easy to run as fast as you can and lower your glove without slowing down. It can be risky, too. If a fielder misses a shoestring catch, the ball might roll all the way to the fence.

Glossary

BASEBALL WORDS TO KNOW

ALL-STAR—A player who is selected to play in baseball's annual All-Star Game.

AMERICAN LEAGUE (AL)—One of baseball's two major leagues. The AL started play in 1901.

CENTRAL DIVISION—One of three groups of teams making up a league. These teams play in the middle section of the country.

CHANGEUP—A slow pitch disguised to look like a fastball.

COMPLETE GAME—A statistic credited to a pitcher who stays in a game from start to finish.

CY YOUNG AWARD—The trophy given to each league's best pitcher each year.

DOUBLEHEADER—Two games scheduled to be played in one day.

EARNED RUN AVERAGE (ERA)—A statistic that measures how many runs a pitcher gives up for every nine innings he pitches.

GOLD GLOVE—An award given each year to baseball's best fielders.

HALL OF FAMER—A player honored as one of the best ever by baseball's Hall of Fame, in Cooperstown, New York.

HOMESTAND—A series of games—often against several teams—held in a team's home stadium.

LINEUP—The list of players who are playing in a game.

MAJOR-LEAGUE—Belonging to the American League or National League, which make up the major leagues.

MINOR-LEAGUE—Belonging to one of the professional baseball leagues at a lower level than the major leagues.

MOST VALUABLE PLAYER (MVP)—An award given each year to each league's top player; an MVP is also selected for the World Series and All-Star Game.

NATIONAL LEAGUE (NL)—The older of the two major leagues. The NL started play in 1876.

PENNANT—A league championship. The term comes from the triangular flag awarded to each season's champion, beginning in the 1870s.

PLAYER-MANAGER—Someone who both plays for and manages a baseball team.

ROOKIE—A player in his first season.

SAVED—Recorded the last out in a team's win. A pitcher on the mound for the last out of a close victory is credited with a "save."

SHUTOUT—A game in which one team does not allow its opponent to score a run.

STANDINGS—A daily list of teams, starting with the team with the best record and ending with the team with the worst record.

SWITCH-HITTER—A player who can hit from either side of home plate. Switch-hitters bat left-handed against right-handed pitchers, and right-handed against left-handed pitchers.

TRIPLE CROWN—An honor given to a player who leads the league in home runs, batting average, and runs batted in.

WORLD SERIES—The world championship series played between the winners of the American and National Leagues.

OTHER WORDS TO KNOW

BLUNDERS—Mistakes.

COMEBACK—The process of catching up from behind, or making up a large deficit.

CONEY ISLAND—A famous amusement park in Brooklyn, New York.

DEFENSIVE BACK—A position on a football team. A defensive back is usually a cornerback or a safety.

EVAPORATE—Disappear, or turn into vapor.

FAVORED—Gave an advantage to.

FLANNEL— A soft wool or cotton material.

INTERLOCKING—Joined in many places.

LOGO—A symbol or design that represents a company or team.

PIGEON-TOED—Walking with the toes pointed inward, like a pigeon.

PROFESSIONAL—Doing a job for money.

SYNTHETIC—Made in a laboratory, not in nature.

TRADITIONAL—Done the same way from generation to generation.

Places to Go

ON THE ROAD

ST. LOUIS CARDINALS
700 Clark Street
St. Louis, Missouri 63102
(314) 345-9600

NATIONAL BASEBALL HALL OF FAME AND MUSEUM
25 Main Street
Cooperstown, New York 13326
(888) 425-5633
www.baseballhalloffame.org

ON THE WEB

THE ST. LOUIS CARDINALS www.stlcardinals.com
- *Learn more about the Cardinals*

MAJOR LEAGUE BASEBALL www.mlb.com
- *Learn more about all the major league teams*

MINOR LEAGUE BASEBALL www.minorleaguebaseball.com
- *Learn more about the minor leagues*

ON THE BOOKSHELVES

To learn more about the sport of baseball, look for these books at your library or bookstore:

- Kelly, James. *Baseball.* New York, New York: DK, 2005.
- Jacobs, Greg. *The Everything Kids' Baseball Book.* Cincinnati, Ohio: Adams Media Corporation, 2006.
- Stewart, Mark and Kennedy, Mike. *Long Ball: The Legend and Lore of the Home Run.* Minneapolis, Minnesota: Millbrook Press, 2006.

Index

PAGE NUMBERS IN **BOLD** REFER TO ILLUSTRATIONS.

The Team

MARK STEWART has written more than 20 books on football, and over 100 sports books for kids. He grew up in New York City during the 1960s rooting for the Yankees and Mets, and now takes his two daughters, Mariah and Rachel, to watch them play in their home state of New Jersey. Mark omes from a family of writers. His grandfather was Sunday Editor of *The New York Times* and his mother was Articles Editor of *The Ladies' Home Journal* and *McCall's*. Mark has profiled hundreds of athletes over the last 20 years. He has also written several books about his native New York, and New Jersey, his home today. Mark is a graduate of Duke University, with a degree in History. He lives with his daughters and wife Sarah overlooking Sandy Hook, New Jersey.

JAMES L. GATES, JR. has served as Library Director at the National Baseball Hall of Fame since 1995. He had previously served in academic libraries for almost fifteen years. He holds degrees from Belmont Abbey College, the University of Notre Dame and Indiana University. During his career Jim has authored several aca-demic articles and has served in an editorial capacity on multiple book, mag-azine and museum publications, and he also serves as host for the Annual Cooperstown Symposium on Baseball and American Culture. He is an ardent Baltimore Orioles fan and enjoys watching baseball with his wife and two children.